Copyright © 2021 by Jared Koyle

All rights reserved. No part of this publication may be reproduced, distributed, or transmitted in any form or by any means, including photocopying, recording, or other electronic or mechanical methods, without the prior written permission of the publisher, except in the case of brief quotations embodied in critical reviews and certain other noncommercial uses permitted by copyright law.
For permission requests, write to the publisher, addressed "Attention: Permissions Coordinator," at the address below.

Alpha Book Publisher
0 Nadine St, Staten Island,
New York, 10304
www.alphapublisher.com

Ordering Information:
Quantity sales. Special discounts are available on quantity purchases by corporations, associations, and others. For details, contact the publisher at the address above.
Orders by U.S. trade bookstores and wholesalers. Visit www.alphapublisher.com/contact-us to learn more.

Printed in the United States of America

For Ivy, Fern, Aspen, & Lily

Long ago in a distant kingdom, there lived three princesses. But they were not ordinary princesses. Each had been turned into a bear by Moldyrocks, the evil queen.

Like most wicked stepmothers, she was jealous of their beauty and kindness and therefore cursed them to remain bears forever.

The three princesses were the sweetest and most talented girls in the kingdom, but fearing for their lives, they fled far away, deep into the forest and lived there peacefully, together in a cave, for many years.

As time passed, an ominous darkness began to overshadow the castle and kingdom. Then one day, a friendly, wise hare approached the princesses. She told them the only way for the darkness to go away, and for the princesses' curse to be broken, was if the princesses returned to the kingdom and defeated the queen.

As a parting gift, the hare gave them each a smooth polished white stone from the river. She told them the stones were magic and would help them, but that each stone could be used only once. After that, it would become like all other lifeless rocks.

As the princesses traveled, they became lost, but were relieved when off in the distance they saw a small cottage. After knocking on the door, a young man opened it. Asking what they needed, the princesses inquired if he had any beds they could sleep in for the night. He told them he did and that one of the beds was his and the other two were for his parents. Sadly, he also shared that the evil queen had taken his father and mother because they had refused to make a mirror for her.

Though saddened by the young man's story, the princesses were very grateful for his kindness. Remembering the magic stones from the friendly and wise hare, they decided to use one of them, hoping it would return happiness to him.

The next morning when the young man awoke, he discovered that the three bears were gone. But to his surprise, his mother and father were home, lying in their beds, though they could not explain how they came to be there.

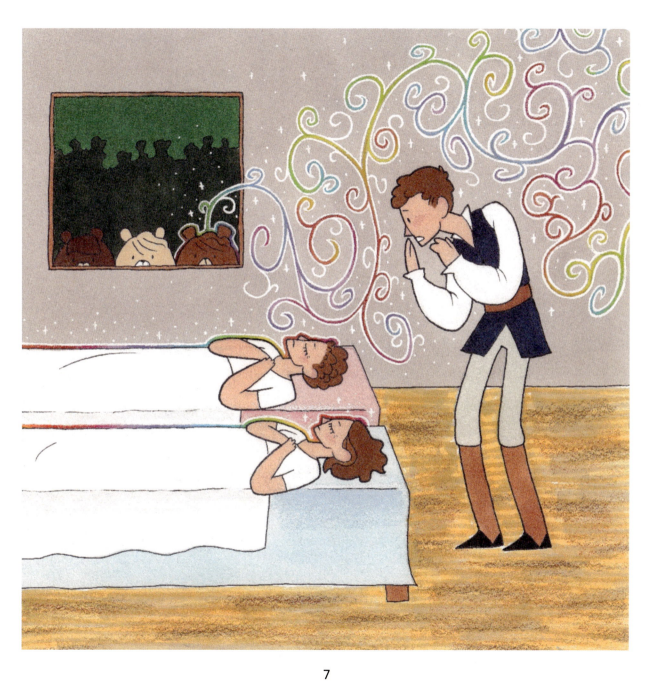

After the princesses had traveled for many hours, they became weary. Just as they were feeling they needed to stop and rest, they noticed chimney smoke coming from a cabin just beyond the next knoll. After knocking on the door, a young maid opened it. Asking what they needed, the princesses inquired if she had any place for them to sit and rest their feet for a while. She told the bears there were three chairs available for them to use. She also told them that one of the chairs was hers and that the other two were for her mother and older brother.

Sadly, she said that her family had refused to build an elaborate wooden frame meant to hold a mirror for the evil queen. So, the queen took her brother and mother away.

While saddened by the young maid's story, the princesses wanted to express their gratitude for her sincere kindness, so they waited for her to go outside to get water from the well. While she was gone, the princesses used another one of the magic stones from the wise hare, with the hope that it too might bring happiness again into the young maid's life.

When she returned with the water, the young maid discovered that the bears were no longer there. But to her amazement, her mother and brother were there, sitting comfortably in their chairs, though they could not explain how they came to be there.

After the bear princesses had eventually traveled a great distance, they began to feel very hungry and weak. Fortunately, just as they were thinking they could go no further, the bears spotted a quaint little cottage not far away and smelled a delicious aroma emitting from the open windows of the cottage. Inside, they could see a beautiful old woman, bent over with age. When the old woman saw them, she smiled and said, "You look hungry!" The princesses each nodded. She then said, "Why don't you come in? I have just finished making the last of my food, but it appears you have more need of it than I do. Please come in!"

Once the princesses were sitting at the old woman's table, she set three small bowls in front of them and proceeded to empty the pot of sweet-smelling porridge into each bowl. As she did the old woman shared how her husband and son were expert rope makers, but that they had been taken by the evil queen in order to make strong ropes for her servants to use to build a large fortress for her castle.

Though saddened by the old woman's tale, the bear princesses were amazed at how she could be so generous and share the last of her food with complete strangers. So, they chose to use the last of the magic stones. Their hope was that happiness might return to the woman in her old age.

The old woman awoke the next morning to find that the three bears were gone. Yet, to her amazement, she saw a heaping pot of hot porridge on the stove and heard the familiar cheerful voices of her husband and son coming up the path to the cottage, though they had no way of explaining when or how they came to be there.

After having traveled a great distance, the three bear princesses discovered their heavy fur had fallen away and all that remained was each beautiful princess in their human form, dressed in the simple and lovely dresses they used to wear before they were cursed as bears. Not only had the magic from the stones returned happiness to those who had shown great kindness to the bears, but after the third wish, the magic of the stones had broken the evil queen's spell, making the princesses human again.

As the princesses approached the borders of the kingdom, they could see how dark and gloomy it had become. It was not yet safe for them to return to the castle, so they purchased a small house just outside of the kingdom's borders and remained there undetected for three years. During that time, they each fell in love and married, not a prince, but a talented young man. The oldest princess married a glass maker. The second married a woodworker. And the youngest married a rope maker.

Together they devised a plan to trick the queen and her army into permanently surrendering the kingdom to the princesses. Their plan was to build a massive magic mirror. When a person looked into the mirror it showed them how they would appear if they chose good instead of evil.

The oldest princess and the glass maker created a mirror as tall as ten castle towers and as long as 1000 wagons that stretched across the length of an entire meadow. The second princess and the woodworker built a beautiful, large, and strong frame that fit perfectly around the mirror. The youngest princess and the industrious rope maker created great cords to be used for lifting the massive mirror into place.

When Moldyrocks learned of the princesses' plan, she assembled her vast dark army for battle. As the evil queen and her army ran quickly toward the princesses in battle, to her surprise she saw facing her what appeared to be an immensely powerful army dressed in white. Convinced she was looking, not at herself, but at the princesses' army, the evil queen Moldyrocks gave the command and led the charge to destroy the great and good army in front of her.

In her anger toward the princesses, the queen redoubled her speed to ensure the force of her army would destroy the enemy and any remaining hope of happiness in the kingdom. What the queen did not see was that the mirror was delicately placed at the very end of the meadow, high on the edge of a cloud covered cliff.

With great speed, Queen Moldyrocks raced toward her rival. Just as she was face to face with the image of her opponent, she gave the command for her army to fire their weapons and defeat the enemy. As they did, the mirror shattered, revealing the terrifying cliffs. But it was too late. The evil queen, with her terrible army, tumbled beneath the clouds, never to be seen or heard from again.

The three princesses restored their kingdom once again to its beauty and grandeur, filled with kindness and happiness. It is rumored the kingdom still exists, but one can only see it through the magic of a mirror.

The End

Made in the USA
Middletown, DE
09 May 2021